Travel Mumbai: Places to Visit in Mumbai

MUMBAI TRAVEL GUIDE

BY

SHALU SHARMA

D1522165

Copyright:

Copyright © 2017 Shalu Sharma. All Rights Reserved.

http://www.shalusharma.com

No portion of this book may be modified, reproduced or distributed mechanically, electronically or by any other means including photocopying without the written permission of the author.

Image cover: Rajabai Clock Tower, © [Malgorzata Kistryn] / Dollar Photo Club

Disclaimer:

Whilst every care is taken to ensure that the information in this book is as up-to-date and accurate as possible, no responsibility can be taken by the author for any errors or omissions contained herein. Responsibility for any loss, damage, accident or distress resulting from adherence to any advice, suggestions or recommendations is not taken.

Other Books by the Author

Essential India Travel Guide: Travel Tips And Practical Information
India Travel Survival Guide For Women
Essential Hindi Words And Phrases For Travelers To India
Hindi Language For Kids And Beginners: Speak Hindi Instantly
India Travel Health Guide: Health Advice and Tips for Travelers to India
Real Ghost And Paranormal Stories From India
India For Kids: Amazing Facts About India

You can connect with her on her social media sites

Twitter: https://twitter.com/bihar
Google Plus: https://plus.google.com/+ShaluSharma1
Pinterest: http://www.pinterest.com/shalusharma
Facebook: https://www.facebook.com/TourIncredibleIndia

Table of contents

The city of Mumbai

Mumbai is the capital city of Maharashtra state of India. Mumbai used to be called Bombay until the name was officially changed in 1995. The city has about 18.4 million people, which makes it the most populous city in all of India. Mumbai is a part of the Mumbai Metropolitan Region. This region is one of the world's most populous urban regions. It is also the second most populous metropolitan area in the country of India. Mumbai can be found on the western coastal region of India. Since it is alongside the waters of the Arabian Sea, it has a deep natural harbor where a lot of commercial fishing and boating takes place. There are also numerous beaches alongside the western shores of the city that are suitable for people who like to swim or get a tan. The white sandy beaches in and around Mumbai are beautiful, especially during the winter seasons.

Mumbai at the break of dawn

Mumbai is the richest city in all of India. You will find the majority of India's billionaires and millionaires living there. It also has the highest gross domestic product of any city in Central Asia, West Asia or South Asia. Mumbai is known as an alpha world city, which basically means it plays a vital role in the global economy. Many Indian corporations in the city do business with other nations of the world. Not only that, Mumbai is also a popular tourist city. This means many foreigners from around the world come to Mumbai to visit the beaches, shop at the stores, eat at the restaurants and stay at the hotels of the city. All of this generates huge amounts of revenue for the Indian economy, which in turn stimulates the growth of Indian businesses that conduct international affairs with foreign nations. As for the foreign tourists coming to India, they like to come to Mumbai because it is a vibrant city with plenty of sites to see. It is also a more pleasant city to look at because it is better developed. If someone were to travel away from Mumbai towards the central region of India, they would find much more poverty stricken people and locations. For this reason, they like to stay in Mumbai in order to make their experience in India more pleasant.

The Gateway of India with the hotel Taj Mahal Palace on the right

Mumbai is the commercial, entertainment and financial capital of the entire Indian country. The Hindi language film industry known as "Bollywood" is located in Mumbai. This makes the city like the American version of "Hollywood," which is the predominate location for filmmaking in the United States. In India, Mumbai is where most of India's major films get produced. The city also caters to other industries as well. It houses many important financial institutions for the country, including the Bombay Stock Exchange, the SEBI, the National Stock Exchange of India and the Reserve Bank of India. Not only that, but numerous companies and multinational corporations based in India are headquartered in Mumbai. Even the scientific institutes of India are based in Mumbai, such as the AECI, TIFR, AERB, NPCL, BARC and the Department of Atomic Energy.

Mahatma Jyotiba Phule Mandai (formerly Crawford Market)

With all of the business opportunities available in Mumbai, it attracts people from all over India and throughout the rest of the world to come to the city to do business there. For the Indian people, the city offers them a higher standard of living than they could find anywhere else in the country. Mumbai contains numerous high paying job opportunities that you won't find anywhere else in India. The city has been nicknamed the "melting pot" because it contains a variety of cultures and communities that come together as one in order to make a better life for themselves.

History of Mumbai

The history of Mumbai can be traced back to 2,000 years ago. For a long time particularly during the British rule, Mumbai was referred to as Bombay. But it wasn't just one big landmass like it is today. Mumbai was originally known as the seven islands of Bombay because it was made up of seven islands grouped closely together on the water, which is known as an "archipelago." These islands were called Mahim, Colaba, Worli, Old Woman's Island, Parel, Mazagaon and Bombay Island.

Inscriptions on the Gateway of India reading "Erected to commemorate the landing in India of

their Imperial Majesties King George V and Queen Mary on the Second of December MCMXI"

Archaeologists and historians are not too sure when these islands were first inhabited by people. However, there have been Pleistocene sediments discovered throughout the coastal areas of northern Mumbai. These sediments make scientists believe that the islands were first inhabited sometime during the Stone Age, which is a pretty vast time period that ranges from 3.4 million B.C. to 6000 B.C.

In 300 B.C., the Bombay islands became part of the Maurya Empire as it expanded down south in India. This Empire was ruled by a powerful king named Ashoka of Magadha. The western region of India became an important Buddhist centre throughout ancient times because of Buddhist emperors. The Kanheri Caves in Borivali and the Mahakali Caves in Andheri were eventually built as Buddhist monasteries. They are located in the western region of Mumbai. The remains of these monasteries still exist today and have become tourist attractions for people interested in the history of Buddhism and the history of India in general. Modern day Buddhists are also free to come to these caves for prayer if they so desire.

Church of Our Lady of Dolours, Wadala. A Roman Catholic church in built in 1853

From 200 B.C. to 800 A.D., the islands of Mumbai came to be ruled by dynasties which were indigenous to the islands. There were the Abhiras, Kalachuris, Satavahanas, Konkan Mauryas, Western Kshatrapas, Vakatakas, Rashtrakutas, and Chalukyas. Later on between 810 and 1260, the Sihara dynasty ruled over the islands. There are many caves on these islands which contain structures and evidence that were built when these dynasties ruled. Like the other two caves mentioned, these were also caves devoted to Buddhism. There were also caves devoted to Hinduism as well, which is another popular religion to come out of ancient India. Some of these other caves include the Jogeshwari Caves from the sixth century, the Elephanta Caves from the seventh century, the Walkeshwar Temple from the 10th century and the Banganga Tank from the 12th century.

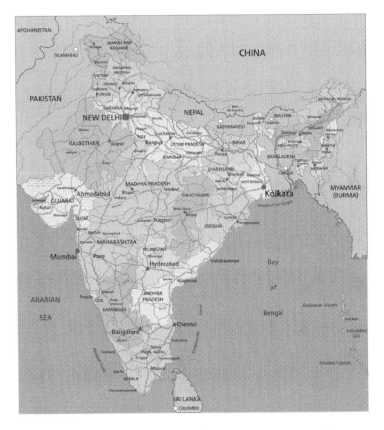

During the 16th century, the Portuguese Overseas Empire discovered a route by sea that would take officials from Portugal to the western coast of the Indian subcontinent. Once this route was discovered, the governing body from Portugal set up colonies and fortresses on the seven islands of Bombay. These islands were eventually handed over to the English government as a dowry after the Portuguese princess named Catherine of Braganza married King Charles II of England. The King rented out the islands in 1668 to the East India Company, which was a joint-stock company involved in trading practices in the East Indies. The company paid the King 10 pounds of gold on a yearly basis to use the islands.

In 1845, a series of land reclamation projects began on the seven islands of Bombay. The goal was to merge the seven islands of Bombay and turn them into one big landmass. This landmass would become Greater Bombay. Once this transformation process was completed, Bombay became one of the biggest seaports to exist on the Arabian Sea. The city started to see educational and economic growth as a result. In the early 20th century, India's Independence movement took place and Bombay became a strong base for this movement. India finally achieved its independence in 1947, which caused Bombay to be turned into Bombay State. But after the Samyukta Maharashtra movement of 1960, a new state called "Maharashtra" was formed and Bombay became its capital.

Getting around Mumbai and transport systems in Mumbai

Mumbai is a city where people rely heavily on public transportation to get around. Of course, people are free to use their own cars if they can afford one. Unfortunately, most people in the city cannot afford their own cars since Mumbai is a very rich and expensive city to the average Indian citizen. So like most cities, you will find an abundance of trains, buses, auto rickshaws and taxis in Mumbai to help you get from place to place. If you are a tourist then you will definitely want to take advantage of these services to get around the city comfortably.

Taxis in Mumbai

15

The easiest and most convenient form of transportation in Mumbai is the taxi services. The black and yellow Fiat metered taxis can be found all over the city. All you have to do is hail one down with your arms if you see one passing you by. Over the years there have been more taxi cab companies opening in Mumbai. Now you will find white and red metered taxis, silver and green taxis, blue and silver taxis and so on. The colors represent the various taxi companies and any special service they provide. For example, the company "Cool Cabs" owns the blue and silver taxis. Their specialty is providing air conditioned taxi cab rides to its passengers, which matches the colors and the name of the company.

The Brihanmumbai Electric Supply and Transport Company have single decker and double decker buses available for people who want to take public bus transportation. For those who want air conditioned buses, you can take the Volvo buses that travel from Navi Mumbai Municipal Transport to Dadar, Borivali and Bandra. If you need to go to Mulund towards the western side of the city, there are non-air conditioned buses available from Navi Mumbai to take you there. Some other bus transit systems in the Mumbai region are Kalyan-Dombivli Municipal Transport operating in Dombivli and Kalyan; Thane Municipal Transport operating in Borivali and Mulund; Mira-Bhayandar Municipal Transport operating in Jogeshwari, Borivali and Mira-Bhayandar; and Vasai-Virar Municipal Transport operating in Mulund and Vasai-Virar. In February of 2014, Mumbai introduced its first monorail line to the people of the city. This system is respectively called Mumbai Monorail. There are still more lines currently being constructed to expand its travel options for people. A rapid transit system named Mumbai Metro also got developed in 2014 to reduce the congestion of traffic within the city.

The railway networks in Mumbai have been around since the 1800s. In fact, the oldest railway in all of Asia is the Mumbai Suburban Railway which was established in 1867. The Indian government operates an enterprise called "Indian Railways," which owns Mumbai Suburban Railway and a number of other railways throughout India.

The Mumbai Suburban Railway is operated by the divisions of Central Railways and Western Railways. The railway transports about 6.3 million people per day, which is over 50% of Indian Railways' daily capacity. This also makes Mumbai Suburban Railway have the highest passenger density out of any other railway in the world. The railway has four radial lines; the Western line that goes between Dahanu Road and Churchgate Railway Station; the Central line that goes between Kasara and Chatrapati Shivaji Terminus; the Harbour line that goes between Panvel and CST; and the Trans-Harbour line that goes between Vashi and Thane.

Other forms of transportation include auto rickshaws and ferry boats. Auto rickshaws are much smaller motor vehicles that tend to get around the city faster. However, they are not allowed to go beyond certain municipal points of Mumbai. As for the ferry boat service, this comes in handy if you have to get to other islands within the region or across the city without having to drive there.

When to visit India

The usual time in which people like to travel the most are during holidays and summer vacations. But when you travel to India you need to consider the weather more than anything else. India experiences frequent monsoons between July to September. This type of weather is a mixture of rain and heavy winds on a regular basis. It is the type of weather where you will want to stay indoors most of time, which wouldn't make the trip very memorable if you are a tourist looking to go sightseeing. That is why the best time to visit India is between late October and late March. This will allow you to avoid the rainy and windy weather conditions. Of course, you will have to endure the colder weather as it gets closer to December and January. Remember that many Indian hotels don't have heated pools or saunas, so you will have to pack your winter clothes to prepare for the cold temperature. If you are looking for weather that is more comfortable then November would be a better time to go.

Once April approaches, the temperature starts to get warm and humid. By the time it gets to be June, the summer temperatures during the daytime typically exceed 100°F. If you are the type of person that loves hot temperatures then you can always go in the summertime. However, if you are coming as a tourist and are going to be exploring a lot of the country then you might get sweaty and tired very fast in this kind of heat. Also, don't forget the monsoon season occurs during the summertime which means you'll have to endure wind and rain on occasion. The monsoon rains tend to start off strong in southern India around April and then move up to northern India as it gets closer to September. It doesn't necessarily rain every single day during this time, but the chances of wind and rain are very high.

You should pay attention to the local weather reports and plan your travel accordingly if you go to Mumbai between these months.

So far we've talked about the comfortable times to go to India where its weather is concerned. Now let's discuss the best time to see cultural or holiday events in India. Remember that India has holidays unique to the country which many foreign tourists are not even aware of. This means you could go to India to see these holidays and not have to worry too much about other tourists overcrowding the experience. The majority of the people attending these holiday festivals will be the Indian people themselves. This will give you the chance to get very familiar with the cultural experiences that India has to offer. For example,

India's Independence Day is on August 15th. It is a day the country celebrates its independence from Great Britain. Other holiday festivals in Mumbai are based more on the country's Buddhist and Hindu traditions. There is the Banganga Music Festival in the first week of January, the Kala Ghoda Festival in the first week of February, the Hindu festival of Holi in March, the Ganesh Chaturthi from the first week of September, the Festival of Nine Nights celebration starting on October 1st (Navratri), and the Festival of Lights (Diwali) around October or November.

Mumbai at night

If you want to go to Mumbai for globally recognized holidays, then consider spending your New Year's Eve celebration at the Pali Beach resort in Mumbai. You'll get to see fireworks exploding into the night's sky at midnight and you'll get to participate in many parties at the resort. For those interesting in seeing independent films, the Mumbai International Film Festival takes place on October 20th. There are screenings of 100 films that come from over 40 countries. So plan your schedule accordingly if any of these celebrations interest you.

Places to eat in Mumbai

When you visit the city of Mumbai for the first time you might be overwhelmed with the variety of restaurants and street vendors offering exotic food that you have probably never had before. On the other hand, you will also find franchised restaurants from the west that you are more familiar with, like McDonalds. However, you should stick with traditional restaurants that come from India if you want to experience India at its best. For example, the Indigo Delicatessen is a popular eatery that contains a variety of foreign and Indian foods. They even have American-style food to make it a comfortable eating experience for tourists. They have spicy BBQ pork burgers, feta and jalapeno burgers, hazelnut ice cream and thin pizzas. This is the city's way of westernizing their restaurant menus. But the west isn't the only region they cater to. You can also find Chinese food at Ling's Pavilion in Colaba. Get a dose of friend pan noodles served with mushroom, beef, garlic, and more. Try their Pork Dim Sum or their homemade soft tofu that melts in your mouth. Any lover of Chinese food will want to check this place out. Colaba is a southern region of Mumbai.

As a tourist or visitor to Mumbai, you may want to be adventurous and try some traditional Indian cuisine. Mumbai is filled with traditional Indian restaurants to give you this opportunity. There is Bademiya in Colaba, Kolya in Colaba, Bademiya Fine Dine Restaurant in Fort, The Fusion Kitchen in Borivali West, The Yellow Chili at Viviana Mall in Majiwada, Oye Kake in Fort and many other Indian eateries. Some of the best food choices you should lookout for are the chicken bhuna rolls, tandoori baby potatoes, Koyla's chicken tikka, and kalmi kabab. These are some of the most recommended dishes in all of Mumbai. The taste should be easily adaptable to foreigners who are not used to eating Indian food. Some of these restaurants even allow you to eat on the roof and have a romantic lunch or dinner with your loved one. Just check to see which restaurants have tables and chairs on top of them and they will likely have this option available to you.

If you are the type of traveler who wants to eat at restaurants which are highly rated, then you should consider eating at the award winning restaurant in Mumbai called "Indigo." Their menu is made up of European-Asian style cuisine that typically caters to more upscale customers, like politicians or celebrities. The design of the restaurant has fine detailing with only minimal colors. Now if you are looking for a fabulous restaurant, try "Koh." This restaurant was created by a world renowned chef named Ian Kittichai. It serves Thai cuisine, which uses only fresh organic ingredients. Over 50% of the meals on the menu do not contain any meat either, which is hard to find in other restaurants throughout the city. The design of Koh is also very bright and colorful. It is supposed to reflect the flavors of the foods that the restaurant serves.

There are plenty of places where you can grab something to eat and drink

As a traveler, you may just be looking for a quick meal to give you the energy to continue on your journey. In these situations, you can purchase food from street vendors all over the city. The good thing about buying street food is that it is much cheaper than restaurant food and you will find a vast amount of diversity in the food choices that are out there. You'll have vendors from all different ethnic and cultural backgrounds selling foods they learned how to make from their heritage. However you must be careful of what you eat because of hygiene issues.

Some street foods of Mumbai that you might consider trying: Vada Pav, Panipuri, bhelpuri, sevpuri, dahipuri, samosa sandwiches, Ragda patties, pav bhaji, chinese bhel, idlis, chaat and masala dosas.

Many smaller restaurants have homemade food that may even taste better than high end restaurants. This will give you a chance to try out a variety of different cultural foods as you journey throughout the city.

Chaat, the popular street food in Mumbai and rest of India

Some addresses:

Address of Indigo Delicatessen: Level 3, Phase 2, R-City Mall, LBS Road, Ghatkopar West, Mumbai, Maharashtra 400086, India. Phone:+91 22 2518 1010

Address of Ling's Pavilion: 18, M.B. Marg, Apollo Bandar, Colaba, Mumbai, Maharashtra 400001, India

Address of Indigo: 4, Mandlik Rd, Colaba, Behidn Taj Mahal Hotel, Mumbai, Maharashtra 400001, India

Koh by Ian Kittichai: Address: Hotel InterContinental, 135, Netaji Subhash Chandra Bose Rd, Churchgate, Mumbai, Maharashtra 400020, India. Phone:+91 22 3987 9999

Places to visit in Mumbai

Here are the best places to visit in Mumbai.

Gateway of India

The Gateway of India is a monument in Mumbai that was built by the British overlooking the Arabian Sea to commemorate the visit of King George V and Queen Mary to India. The Governor of Bombay Sir George Sydenham Clarke laid down the monument's first foundation in 1911 and was finally completed in 1924. After it was built, it served as a landing dock for the viceroys and governors when they arrived in India. You can absorb the scenery, eat street food and even go on boats from there to Elephanta Caves. Gateway of India is close to the famous Taj Mahal Palace hotel.

The monument is similar to the one in Delhi (India Gate) and people get confused with the two monuments. There is no entry fee and is open 24 hours.

Address: Gateway of India, Apollo Bandar, Colaba, Mumbai

Marine Drive

The Marine Drive is a C-shaped 4.5km long boulevard from Nariman Point to Babulnath and Malabar Hill in South Mumbai. This boulevard is lined with palm trees with the Chowpatty Beach at the northern end. You will find expensive hotels dotting the drive some of which include the Oberoi, Hilton Tower, The Intercontinental, Hotel Marine Plaza and Sea Green Hotel. It is one of the best places in Mumbai for a walk and to observe the atmosphere of this great city and enjoy the Mumbai skyline. At night the place is lit up and looks magical. You will find a lot of people just simply walking with their friends and family. It is a great spot for photos as well.

Address: Marine Drive Jogging Track, Chowpatty, Girgaon, Mumbai

Siddhivinayak Temple (Mandir)

The Siddhivinayak Mandir (temple) is the richest temple of Mumbai. It is thought that about 1.5 to 2.5 million dollars are donated to this temple every year. This Hindu temple is dedicated to Lord Ganesha, the god of obstacles. The devotees are of the view that if you ask for a wish, it is bound to come true. The temple is so famous that Indian politicians and film stars also visit this temple to get blessings from Lord Ganesha. You can book your "darshan" or visit by visiting their website.

Please note that certain days of the week particularly on Tuesdays, Saturdays, Sundays and some Bank holidays are very crowded. If you can, try to avoid going there on those days.

Address: SK Bole Marg, Prabhadevi, Mumbai.
Phone: +91 22 2437 3626

Chowpatty Beach

The Chowpatty Beach is one of the most popular of all the beaches of Mumbai. It is next to the Marine Drive. It is here where most of the Ganesh Chaturthi celebrations take place and where people immerse their Ganesha idols in the sea. It is quite a spectacle during these celebrations. It is also one of the best places to eat street food specific for Mumbai some of which include pav bhaji, panipuri, bhelpuri and ragda patties. I would like to say that it's not a particularly tidy beach so do expect some litter. But would like to inform you that it is maintained as there are lots of garbage bins and people are now becoming aware of not throwing litter. In addition, it does get crowded and is noisy particularly during the evenings when a lot of people descend down to take a walk on the beach. But overall, it is a nice place for a walk and to enjoy the spirit of Mumbai. So take a stroll along Chowpatty and admire the lovely views across the ocean.

Juhu Beach

Juhu is an affluent suburb of Mumbai that has a very attractive beach. The mornings and evenings are the best time to visit this place. During the evenings you will be able to enjoy the local street food and do horse riding along the beach. You might find it dirty compared to other beaches but nonetheless it's still worth going and enjoying the atmosphere it has to offer.

Elephanta Caves

The Elephanta Caves is a very exciting place to
visit. They are a network of Buddhist and Hindu
caves on an island called Elephanta Island in
Mumbai Harbour in the Arabia Sea. The majority
of the caves are Hindu caves that have stone
sculptures dedicated to Lord Shiva thought to be
made between 5th and 8th centuries. In order to
go to these caves you will need to go to Elephanta
Island. You can get there by ferry or boat from
the Gateway of India that takes about an hour.
You can buy tickets from the Maharashtra tourism
development Corp (MTDC) at the entrance of
Gateway of India. The first boat leaves at 9 in the
morning. It will be a great day out. You can hire a
guide or you can tour the island and the caves

yourself. One thing to remember is that there are lots of free monkeys around so be careful. Try to take your own food and water if you can. You won't be allowed to stay overnight as it's not permitted.

Haji Ali Mosque

Although India is a Hindu dominated country, it has a large Muslim population. A mosque called Haji Ali Dargah is a very popular religious place for Muslims. However Hindus too visit the place in large numbers. It is thought that Sayyed Pir Haji Ali Shah Bukhari of Bukhara (in Uzbekistan) was a very rich merchant but he gave all his possessions away and travelled to Mecca and then around the world finally settling in Mumbai. The Mogul styled complex houses the tomb of Pir Haji Ali Shah Bukhari. The complex also has a mosque called the Haji Ali Masjid. One unique feature of this monument that it has been has built on an islet 500 metres from the coast. If you are religiously or spiritually minded then you could consider visiting this place. You can only get to the mosque during low tide as the causeway is covered with water during the high tides. You can visit this place from 10 am to 10 pm and is free to enter.

Address: Dargarh Road, Lala Lajpat Rai Marg, Mumbai. Phone: +91-22-23529082

Official website: http://hajialidargah.in

Kanheri Caves

The Kanheri Caves are situated in the forests of
the Sanjay Gandhi National Park on the outskirts
of Mumbai. They are considered as the lungs of
the city. There are about 109 caves that served
as Buddhist monasteries. They were carved out of
basalt that have been dated from the first century
BCE to the 10th century CE. You don't have to be
religious to admire these caves. It's easy to get to
these caves and you will have to pay an entry fee
of Rupees 100 if you are a foreign tourist or
Rupees 5 if you are Indian. You could spend the
whole day there or a few hours depending on how
interesting you find the place but it's worth a visit.
They are open every day from 7:30 AM - 5:00
PM.

Address: Sanjay Gandhi National Park, Borivali East, Mumbai

The Rajabai Clock Tower

The Rajabai Clock Tower in 1905

The Venetian and Gothic styled Rajabai Clock Tower is something that resembles a Big Ben. Located in the campus of Mumbai University the building was actually modelled on Big Ben in 1869 by an English architect called Sir George Gilbert Scott. This heritage clock was funded by someone called Premchand Roychand, a rich broker who founded the Bombay Stock Exchange on the condition that the tower would be named after his mother Rajabai. During the British rule of India the tower used to play the tunes of God Save the King, Rule Britannia, A Handel Symphony and Home Sweet Home. At the moment it chimes just one tune every 15 minutes.

You might wish to check out this building as it's free to visit and it should take you half to one hour the most. You can actually see the building from the Oval Maidan (field) exactly opposite of the Rajabai Clock Tower.

Address: Next to the High Court, Fort Campus, Karmaveer Bhaurao Patil Marg, Fort, Mumbai.

Global Vipassana Pagoda

This Pagoda is a Buddhist meditation hall. People of all religious denominations come to this place to meditate. It's very close to EsselWorld so you could combine the trip. There are no entry fees. You can even book a 10-day Vipassana courses but you will need to book them in advance by visiting this website http://www.dhamma.org/en/index.

Address: Next to Esselworld, Gorai Village, Borivali West, Mumbai: Phone: +91 22 3374 7501

Official website: http://www.globalpagoda.org

Dharavi Slum

The area of Dharavi has the largest slum in the world. It might seem odd to visit a slum but it's worth visiting this place to get an idea of how some people live. It's something that you saw in the Slumdog Millionaire movie! It's an experience that will remain with your forever. Here's an interesting fact, Dharavi produces excellent leather goods that gets exported around the world. You will be able to buy premium leather goods here at great prices. But the fact is that it's one poor colony where people who cannot afford flats or houses live in this place. The media and the world are guilty of selling this place to tourists as a bustling place, full of exciting people, narrow lanes, paradise for cheap goods, great people and so on but reality is that people who live here are very poor and is full of dreadful poverty and squalor.

Travel agents are carrying out various kinds of tours of Dharavi but a great way to explore is by a bicycle tour. You will get a guide who will take you around. Just ask you travel agent or your hotel and they will arrange it for you.

Mahalaxmi Dhobi Ghat - Mumbai's Laundry

If you want to see something spectacular then I suggest you take a trip down to Mahalaxmi Dhobi Ghat or simply called the Dhobi Ghat. It is an open air manual laundry where clothes are washed by people called "dhobis". There are more than 5000 of these dhobis (or laundrymen) who wash about 100,000 cloths per day by beating them on the 731 purpose built washing stones. As a foreign tourist it might seem strange to see men washing linen in the open but it is quite a sight.

Address: Dhobi Ghat, Shanti Nagar, Lower Parel, Mumbai

Other places to visit in Mumbai

Hanging Gardens

These are hanging gardens on the top of Malabar Hills. You will be able to see the sunset over the Arabian Sea. It's a great place to walk and enjoy the hedges that are shaped in the form of animals. There are no entry fees. It should take you about an hour or two.

Address: Hanging Garden, Simla Nagar, Malabar Hill, Mumbai

Chhatrapati Shivaji Maharaj Vastu Sangrahalaya (Previously called Prince of Wales Museum)

This is the main museum of Mumbai. Here you will find a great collection of art, sculptures and coins of India and houses excellent artefacts displaying Indian history. It also has a natural history section, archaeology section, a textile galley, a maritime heritage gallery and a miniature painting gallery. If you are a museum fan then this is certainly a place worth visiting.

Address: 159-161, Mahatma Gandhi Road, Kala Ghoda, Fort, Mumbai. Phone: +91 22 2284 4484

Taraporewala Aquarium

This is one of the oldest aquarium and the finest

in India. If you love wildlife and love to see these kinds of things then you should definitely visit this place. If you have children then take them there; they will love it. The tickets cost around Rupees 60 and are valid for only one hour.

Address: Taraporewala Building, Near Charni Road Railway Station, Charni Road, Girgaon, Mumbai. Phone: +91 22 2282 1239

EsselWorld

EsselWorld is a theme and amusement park. It has rides for all ages. If you have children then you could certainly take them to this place. One of the popular rides is the "Monsters In The Mist", India's first scary ride.

Address: Global Pagoda Road, Gorai Island, Borivali West, Mumbai: Phone: +91 22 6528 0305

Official website: http://www.esselworld.in

Kamala Nehru Park

If you fancy a walk in the park then why not visit the well maintained Kamala Nehru Park located in Malabar Hill. The park covers an area of 4000 square feet. It's a popular park amongst the locals. You will get an excellent view of the Marine Drive from this place. There are no entry fees.

Address: B.G. Kher Road, Malabar Hill, Mumbai. Phone: +91-22-23633561

Mount Mary Church, Bandra

If want to visit a Roman Catholic church then you might wish to visit the Mount Mary Church, a Basilica located in Bandra. Some people claim that it has miraculous powers.

Address: Mount Mary, Bandra West, Mumbai

Forts in and around Mumbai

If you are interested in visiting forts in and around Mumbai then here's a list. Click on the hyperlink to see maps and photos.

Bombay Castle – one of the oldest defence structures built by the British to defend the city.

Bassein Fort – a fort situated in the village of Vasai, a suburb of Mumbai.

Belapur Fort – a fort in Belapur in New Bombay (called Navi Mumbai by the locals).

Castella de Aguada (Bandra Fort) – a fort built by the Portuguese as an outpost.

Dongri Hill Fort – a fort located in the Dongri area of Mumbai.

Fort George, Bombay – fortified walls built in 1769 by the British.

Ghodbunder Fort - a fort built by the Portuguese located in Ghodbunder Village, Thane.

Madh Fort – a small fort on Madh Island built by the Portuguese.

Mahim Fort – a British port located in Mahim Bay. The origins are disputed.

Mazagon Fort – a fort built by the British in Mazagaon around 1680.

Riwa Fort – a fort in central Mumbai on the banks of River Mithi.

Sewri Fort – A fort built by the British in 1680 as a watch tower overlooking Mumbai harbour.

Sion Hillock Fort – a fort built by the East Indian Company to mark the boundary between British Parel Island and Portuguese Salsette Island.

Worli Fort – a fort built by the British around 1675 overlooking Mahim Bay.

Places to shop in Mumbai

Here's a list of some popular malls and markets in Mumbai. Click on the hyperlink to see maps and photos.

Chor Bazaar – a large flea market located near Bhendi Bazaar in South Mumbai.

Colaba Causeway – excellent place to buy antiques along with anything you can think of.

Crossroads Mall – a shopping mall in Carmichael Road, Tardeo.

Dava Bazaar – a place where you can buy anything to do with medical and scientific instruments along with chemicals.

Fashion Street – a great place to buy clothes.

Growel's 101 – a shopping mall with food court in Kandivali.

High Street Phoenix – one of the largest shopping malls in India.

Inorbit Mall – an exciting mall that houses food court and 26 restaurants.

Korum Mall – a shopping mall full of branded shops located in Thane in the suburb of Mumbai.

Lamington Road – considered as the IT hub of Mumbai. The markets on this road have excellent shops for computer goods.

Linking Road – one of the main shopping centres on the suburbs of Mumbai.

Lohar Chawl – you can find the best of electrical goods here.

Mahatma Jyotiba Phule Mandai – this is South Mumbai's most famous market. It is closed on Sundays.

Metro Junction Mall – another shopping mall located in located in Kalyan.

Neptune Magnet Mall – a huge shopping mall in shopping mall in Bhandup comprising 6 towers of 22 stories each.

Princess Street –if you are after medically related stuff or surgical equipments then this is the place you should be going.

R City Mall - a shopping mall located in Ghatkopar.

R Mall - a shopping mall situated in Mulund and Thane.

Raghuleela Mall, Kandivili - a mall situated in Kandivali in the suburb of Mumbai.

Raghuleela Mall, Vashi - a mall situated in Vashi, Navi Mumbai.

Viviana Mall, Thane – one of the finest malls in Mumbai.

Important numbers and contacts

Emergency Number: 100

Heart Attack: 105

Fire & Rescue: 101

Ambulance service: 102 / 1298

Tourist Police: 022 2262 1855

Emergency Number (Mumbai): 101, 3085991

Emergency Number (Thane): 101, 5331600

Emergency Number (Vashi): 101, 7660101

Municipal Ambulance   : 3077324

Parsi Ambulance: 3621666

Private Hospitals

Jaslok Hospital

15 Dr Deshmukh Marg, Pedder Road, Mumbai 400026 - Tel: 022 2353 3333

Hiranandani Hospital

Opposite Hiranandani Knowledge Park, Powai Kailash Complex link Road, Hiranandani Gardens, Powai, Mumbai - Tel: 022 2576 3300

Kokilaben Dhirubhai Ambani Hospital

Rao Saheb Achutrao Patwardhan Marg, Four
Bunglows, Andheri West, Mumbai 400053 - Tel:
022 3099 9999

Lilavati Hospital Bandra

791 Bandra Reclamation, Mumbai 400050 - Tel:
022 2675 1000

Sterling Wockhard

Sion Panvel Express Hwy, Sector 7, Vashi, Navi
Mumbai 400703 - Tel: 022 6680 4444

Local words and phrases

The local language of Mumbai is Marathi but Hindi is very popular therefore it's best to memorise Hindi words and phrases which can be used in and outside of Mumbai and other parts of India.

Hello – Namaste

Thank you – Dhanyevad

See you later – Phir milengay

No – Nahi

Yes – Ha

Help - Madad

My name is John – Mera naam John hai

What is your name – Aap ka naam kya hai

How are you – Aap kaise hai

What do you do – Aap kya karte hai

I am from the USA – Mai USA say hu

Where is my room – Mera kamra kaha hai

Where is the hotel – Hotel kidhar hai

Can you take me there – Kya aap mujhe udhar lay jaa saktay hai

How do I get there - Mai udhar kasai jaa sakta hu (male), Mai udhar kaise jaa sakti hu (female)

Where is the hospital – Hospital kidhar hai

Where can I find a taxi – Taxi kidhar milega

How much is this – Ye kitnay ka hai

Can you help me – Kya aap meri madad kar sakte hai

Where should I go – Mujhe kaha jaana hai

Thank you

Thank you for buying this book. I hope you will enjoy your visit to Mumbai. If you have any questions then feel free to visit my website http://shalusharma.com or send me an email at pyt@shalusharma.com.

Here's a list of other books that you might consider buying for your travels to India.

Travel Guides

Essential India Travel Guide: Travel Tips And Practical Information
India Travel Survival Guide For Women
India Travel Health Guide: Health Advice and Tips for Travelers to India
Travel Delhi: Places to Visit in Delhi
Travel India: Enjoying India to the Fullest: Things to do in India

Learn Hindi

Essential Hindi Words And Phrases For Travelers To India
Hindi Language For Kids And Beginners: Speak Hindi Instantly
For the kids

India For Kids: Amazing Facts About India
Mahatma Gandhi For Kids And Beginners
Life and Works of Aryabhata
All about India: Introduction to India for Kids
Mother Teresa of Calcutta: Life of Mother Teresa

Religion

Hinduism For Kids: Beliefs And Practices
Indian Religions For Kids
Religions of the World for Kids
Buddhism Made Easy: Buddhism for Beginners and Busy People

Others

Real Ghost And Paranormal Stories From India

If you have any questions then feel free to email me on pyt@shalusharma.com or you can subscribe to my emails for updates, free books and deals here http://www.shalusharma.com/subscribe.

Image credits:

Map of India (Showing Mumbai): © [pbardocz] / Dollar Photo Club

Marine Drive in Mumbai: © [Matyas Rehak] / Dollar Photo Club

Global Vipassana Pagoda Photo: © [saiko3p] / Dollar Photo Club

Dharavi Slum Photo: © [flocu] / Dollar Photo Club

Thank you and enjoy your stay in Delhi

###